Shohei Ohtani

LA
Dodgers
17

Shohei Ohtani

Erin Silver

Living in THE SPOTLIGHT

CREATIVE EDUCATION
CREATIVE PAPERBACKS

Published by Creative Education and Creative Paperbacks
P.O. Box 227, Mankato, Minnesota 56002
Creative Education and Creative Paperbacks are imprints of The Creative Company
www.thecreativecompany.us

Book design by Graham Morgan (www.bluedes.com)
Art direction by Tom Morgan

Images by Getty Images/Alex Trautwig, 23, Brian van der Brug, 29, Chris Bernacchi/Diamond Images, 2, Daniel Shirey, cover, 6–7, David Crane/MediaNews Group/Los Angeles Daily News, 37, Gina Ferazzi, 34, JC Olivera/Variety, 44, JIJI PRESS, 13, 17, Keith Birmingham/MediaNews Group/Pasadena Star-News, 32–33, Leonard Ortiz/MediaNews Group/Orange County Register, 26, MediaNews Group/Orange County Register, 20, Yuki Taguchi, 19; Wikimedia Commons/Erik Drost, 4–5, Joe Glorioso/All-Pro Reels, cover, 9, 10, 14, 31, 41, Joyce N. Boghosian/The White House, 25, Moto "Club4AG" Miwa, 38, shi.k, 45, 内閣官房内閣広報 Cabinet Secretariat Public Relations Office, 46

Every effort has been made to contact copyright holders for material reproduced in this book. Any omissions will be rectified in subsequent printings if notice is given to the publisher.

Library of Congress Cataloging-in-Publication Data
Names: Silver, Erin, 1980- author
Title: Shohei Ohtani / by Erin Silver.
Description: Mankato, Minnesota : Creative Education and Creative Paperbacks, [2026] | Series: Living in the spotlight | Includes bibliographical references and index. | Audience: Ages 10-14 | Audience: Grades 7-9 | Summary: "Get to know baseball star Shohei Ohtani in this sports biography that showcases his athletic achievements with Major League Baseball, personal challenges, and personal life. Written for middle-grade readers, it includes table of contents, sidebars, glossary, resources, and index"– Provided by publisher.
Identifiers: LCCN 2025021343 (print) | LCCN 2025021344 (ebook) | ISBN 9798895811306 library binding | ISBN 9798896800835 paperback | ISBN 9798895812563 ebook
Subjects: LCSH: Ohtani, Shohei, 1994- | Baseball players–Japan–Biography | Pitchers (Baseball)–Biography | Batting (Baseball)–Juvenile literature | Los Angeles Angels of Anaheim (Baseball team) | Los Angeles Dodgers (Baseball team) | Baseball–Japan–History, Local | Baseball–California–History, Local | LCGFT: Biographies
Classification: LCC GV865.O42 S55 2026 (print) | LCC GV865.O42 (ebook) | DDC 796.357092 [B]–dc23/eng/20250626
LC record available at https://lccn.loc.gov/2025021343
LC ebook record available at https://lccn.loc.gov/2025021344

Printed in the United States

LA
GUGGENHEIM

CONTENTS

Introduction

It's September 19, 2024. Shohei Ohtani, number 17 for the Los Angeles Dodgers, steps up to the plate. It's a big game for the 6-foot-4, 210-pound (1.93-meter, 95-kilogram) phenom from Japan. He not only wants to help his team make it to the playoffs, but also wants to make history. He is two home runs and one stolen base short of becoming the first person to hit 50 home runs and steal 50 bases in one season.

In his first at bat, Shohei hits a double. Then he steals third base—his 50th of the year. In the second inning, he steals another. In the sixth, he homers—number 49—and puts the Dodgers ahead of the Miami Marlins. The next inning—*smack!*—Shohei homers again. Number 50! Screaming fans get to their feet. Shohei jogs around the bases, smiling wide. At home plate, his coaches and teammates laugh, hug, high-five, and pat Shohei on the back. Shohei waves to the fans, who cheer even louder.

By the end of the game, Shohei has hit two doubles, a single, and two home runs, and he's stolen two bases. It is one of the best games by any baseball player in history. Sports reporters call Shohei "extraordinary." They say he's a "unique human" and call him the G.O.A.T.—the greatest of all time. They say Shohei has already earned his spot in the National Baseball Hall of Fame. But his major-league career is just getting started.

G
GUGGENHEIM

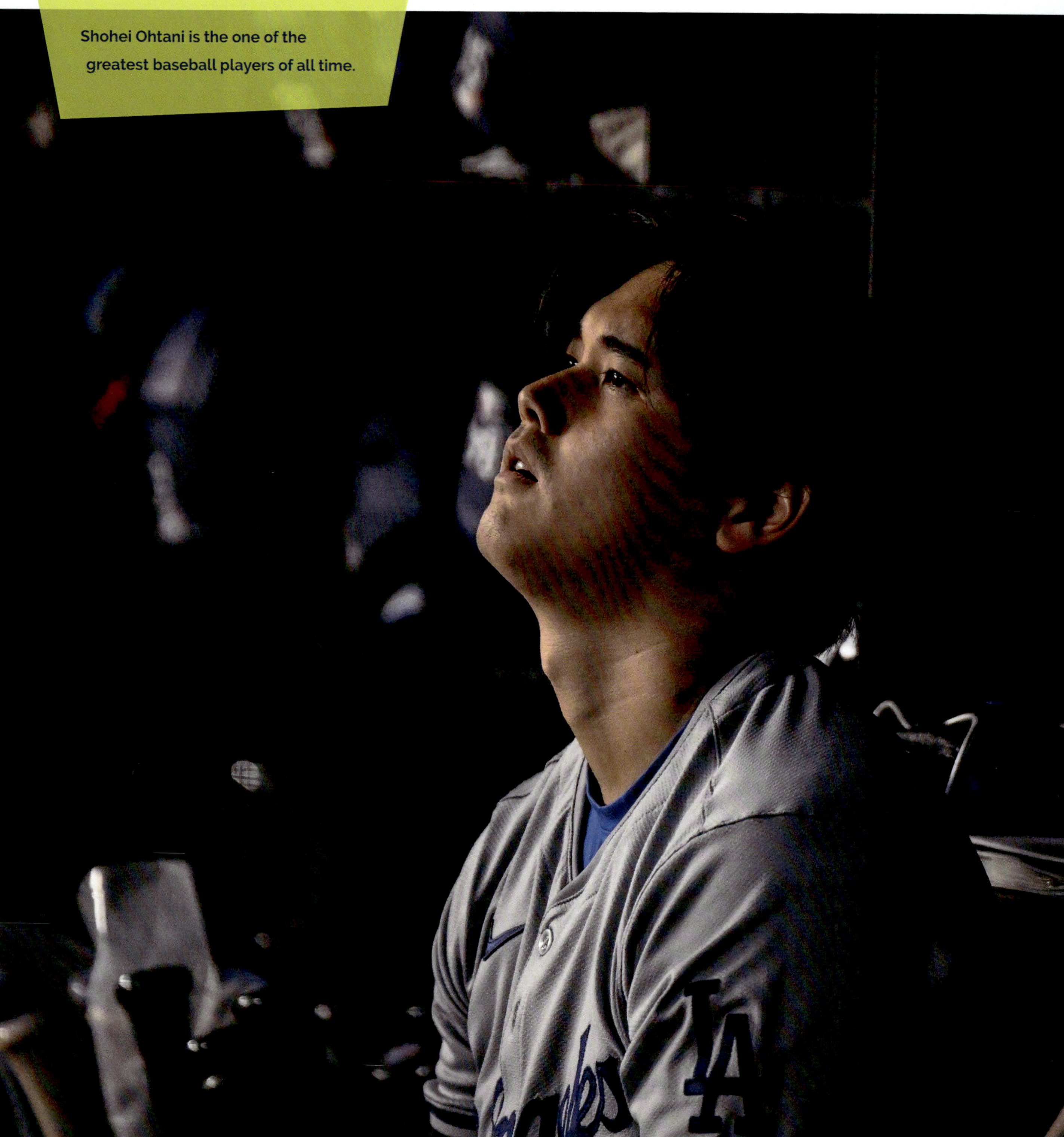

Shohei Ohtani is the one of the greatest baseball players of all time.

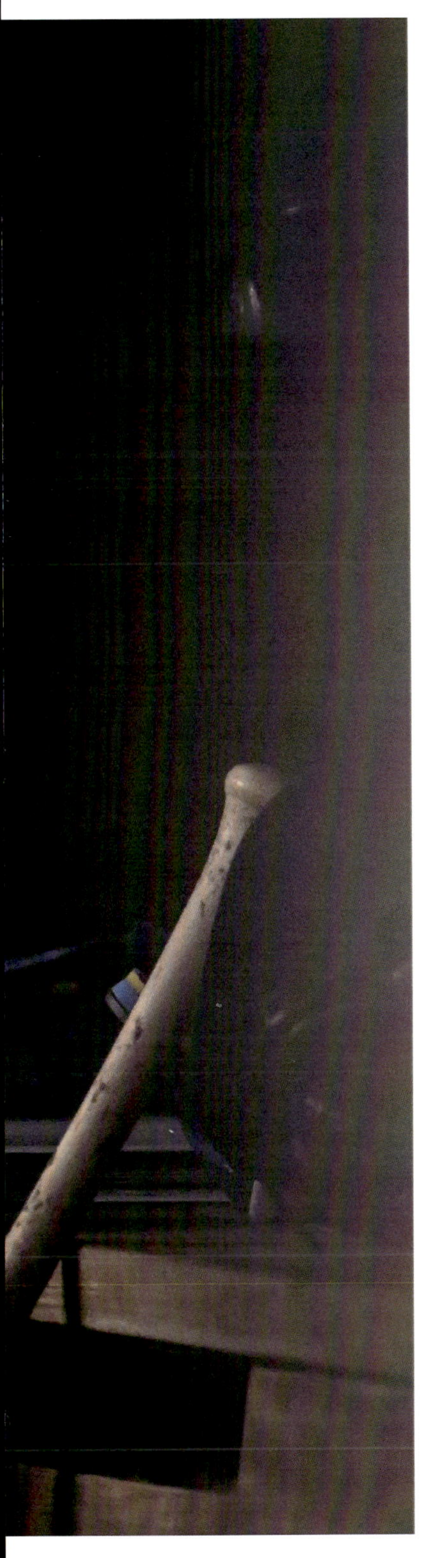

CHAPTER 1:

Yakyū Shōnen

Shohei Ohtani was born on July 5, 1994, in Mizusawa, Japan, about 300 miles (481.8 km) from Tokyo. He grew up in the countryside, surrounded by farmland and mountains, in a family of athletes. Shohei's father, Toru, was a semiprofessional baseball player. His mother, Kayoko, played badminton at the national level. His older sister, Yuka, played volleyball, and his older brother, Ryuta, played baseball.

But Shohei didn't start out playing baseball. "I liked both badminton and swimming," he said, "but baseball was the first thing I thought looked cool, and I had the most confidence in it."

When Shohei was in second grade, his parents signed him up to play on his first baseball team. From that moment on, he knew he wanted to be a baseball player when he grew up. He loved the sport so much that friends and family called him *yakyū shōnen*, or "baseball boy," because he spent all day playing baseball and all night dreaming about it. Baseball was Shohei's life.

Shohei was naturally good at baseball, but he also practiced—a lot. He spent as much time as possible playing baseball with his dad. On evenings and weekends, when Toru wasn't working at the Mitsubishi car factory, they went to a baseball diamond to hit and throw. Toru even managed his son's elementary school team and coached him in junior high. He wanted to teach his son everything he knew.

Toru explained, "When Shohei's older brother was playing, I was too busy with work to teach him how to play baseball. I couldn't even play catch with him," he said regretfully. "Because of that, I was determined to teach Shohei baseball as hard as I could."

Shohei's dad taught him the importance of hard work. "My father thought that if there was a kid who was as good as me, he would send him to the games, not me," said Shohei. "So, for me to play in the games, I had to have overwhelming ability. I had to be good enough to convince everyone on the team. I was still small, but I understood that. I thought I should practice more than anyone else."

In elementary school, Shohei kept a baseball notebook. Toru wrote his feedback and advice in it each day, and Shohei added his own thoughts and ideas for improvement. "I thought the important thing was that when he had a bad day, he would think about what he could do next to overcome the issue and put it into action," said Toru.

But Shohei's parents made sure their son didn't play too much. They didn't want him to get tired of baseball or get injured. They wanted baseball to be fun for him. They were happy when Shohei

18-year-old Hanamaki Higashi High School student Shohei pitches in 2012.

ZOOM IN: FOR THE LOVE OF BASEBALL

The phrase *yakyū shōnen* is Japanese for "baseball boy." Shohei explained, "Yakyū shōnen is a kid who loves baseball, who's just purely enjoying baseball. When I was a yakyū shōnen . . . all the practices were usually on the weekend, so I was waiting all week for the weekend to hurry up and come so I could practice and play some ball." Today, fans can still see how much Shohei loves the sport. He smiles when he does something great. He plays his hardest and with joy. And he looks like he's excited to play every game.

took breaks. "He would concentrate on practice," said Kayoko, "but during breaks, he would play more happily than anyone else. He would splash water with his teammates if they had a hose, or play golf with a ball and bat."

This approach paid off. Shohei's Little League coach, Shoji Asari, remembered the time Shohei competed in a home run competition. He hit 11 balls over the fence to win the championship, and Shoji realized Shohei had the potential to become a professional player one day.

Shohei worked hard to be the best he could. And he had one unique ability: He was a two-way (dual) player. He was a great pitcher *and* a great hitter—something that's very rare in baseball.

Shohei, who throws right-handed and bats left-handed, explained, "I started playing baseball not really thinking I want to be a great player as a pitcher, or I want to be a great player as a hitter. I want to bat well. I want to pitch well. That's the desire I've always had."

Shohei attended a high school known for its baseball program. In addition to his studies, he focused on strength, mental toughness, nutrition, and throwing as fast as a professional player. By his last year of high school, Shohei could throw a fastball at 99.4 miles

(160 kilometers) per hour, up from 93.2 miles (150 km) per hour in his second year. He could also run to first base in 3.8 seconds, a blazing speed. When one of his big games was on TV, baseball fans noticed his skill. Many professional baseball scouts in Japan wanted to sign Shohei to their teams when he graduated from high school. But Shohei wanted to be the first Japanese player to jump from high school straight to the American big leagues. Baseball fans wondered: Would Shohei change his mind and stay in Japan to play baseball for Nippon Professional Baseball (NPB)? Or would the rising star move to the United States to play **Major League Baseball (MLB)** instead?

It was a tough decision for an 18-year-old. But in 2013, he signed with an NPB team called the Hokkaido Nippon-Ham Fighters when they agreed to let him be a hitter and a pitcher. So Shohei moved into the team's dorm in Sapporo, Japan, and focused on his baseball goals. He'd decided to have patience and develop as a dual player before reaching for his ultimate goal: MLB.

Shohei did well in NPB. In 2016, he was named the NPB Pacific League's best pitcher and its best **designated hitter**. He helped his team win a Pacific League championship and **Japan Series** title. He even won the home run derby. Everyone, from fans to scouts to reporters, was impressed with Shohei's one-in-a-million talent.

He's easily the best player I've ever seen," said a sports journalist who covers the NPB. "Every time you watch Ohtani, he makes you think he might do something you have never seen."

ZOOM IN: DUAL PLAYERS

Before Shohei, there hadn't been a well-known dual player since Babe Ruth—about 100 years earlier. It's so difficult to be a good pitcher *and* a good hitter that hardly anybody in the big leagues has even tried. When Shohei wanted to both pitch and hit, teams worried he would injure himself or that his attention would be split, and he wouldn't succeed at either. Shohei proved everyone wrong. In his five years with NPB, he was named best pitcher, best designated hitter, and Most Valuable Player (MVP). By 2018, MLB was willing to let Shohei be a designated hitter and pitcher.

Shohei pitches for the Nippon Ham Fighters in 2015.

During his five years with the Fighters, from age 18 to 22, Shohei became more and more famous. Soon, he couldn't walk around in public without fans screaming for his picture. The media followed him everywhere, too.

Then, the moment Shohei had been waiting for all his life arrived. After the 2017 NPB season, Shohei was ready to move on to MLB, baseball's highest level. But what team would he play for? Would anyone let him both pitch and hit? And with expectations so high, how would Shohei perform under MLB stadium lights? The baseball world couldn't wait to find out.

Shohei is a dedicated teammate and enjoys giving back to communities.

CHAPTER 2:

It's Sho-time

While playing in Japan for the Fighters, Shohei quickly developed into a leading hitter and pitcher—and he was years younger than everyone else. Because of his rare talent as a dual player, people even called him Japan's Babe Ruth. It was a huge compliment.

"[Babe Ruth's] like a mythical character to me," said Shohei. "Because it's such a long time ago and he was God to baseball. I shouldn't be compared to him, at least not right now."

But after a great season in 2017, Shohei was ready to follow in Ruth's footsteps and play at the highest level: He asked to be **posted** to MLB. Shohei was excited to see how his 102-mile-per-hour (164.2 km/h) fastball would do against top hitters like two-time **National League** MVP Bryce Harper. He also wondered how he'd hit against pitchers like Clayton Kershaw, a three-time winner of the **Cy Young Award** for best MLB pitcher. "Just thinking about facing

JAPAN

ANGELS
ANGELS
ANGELS
CBC

ZOOM IN: HIGHLIGHTS

Shohei set so many records in 2024, it's impossible to list them all. Here are a few:

- He was the sixth player to hit 40 home runs and steal 40 bases to join the 40-40 club.
- He's the only member of the 50-50 club.
- With 225 home runs in MLB, he has the most of any player born in Japan.
- He was the first player to finish in the top five of six baseball statistical categories in one year. He led MLB in runs; was second in home runs, **RBIs**, and stolen bases; and fourth in hits and walks.

23-year-old Shohei at a press conference for the Los Angeles Angels.

him makes me really happy and excited," said Shohei about Kershaw. "I could just tell he's such a great pitcher through the TV screen."

The Fighters were sad to see him go, but they knew it was time. "For our team, we're all for him going to the States," said team manager Hideki Kuriyama. "It's going to hurt. It's tough that way. But more than that, I want him to succeed."

Every MLB team wanted Shohei. He met with all of them. He wanted to know their plan for using him as a dual player. He narrowed his list down to seven teams. When he finally chose a team, people were shocked. It was the Los Angeles Angels, who weren't a successful team. They hadn't made the playoffs since 2014. But Shohei was confident the Angels would give him the best chance to do something nobody had done in a century. They even met with his former coaches in Japan to learn how often he should pitch. They asked whether Shohei should hit on days he pitched.

During Shohei's first spring training in Arizona, scouts came out to watch him in action. They wondered if he would live up to the hype. They thought he should test his skills in the minor leagues first. But Shohei had other ideas. During his first MLB game in 2018, he swung at his very first pitch and got a hit. Three days later, Shohei struck out six batters with a 99-mile-per-hour (159.3 km/h) fastball to earn his first win as a pitcher. Then, in his first appearance at his home stadium, Shohei hit his first home run. It was Sho-time.

Unfortunately, Shohei's success as a dual player didn't last long. By June, he was injured. He had a strained elbow and couldn't pitch for the rest of the season. The good news? Shohei finished the year with 22 home runs, 61 runs batted in (RBIs), and an on-base plus slugging percentage (**OPS**) of .925, making him one of the best sluggers in the league. That year he won the **American League (AL)** Rookie of the Year Award.

Shohei's elbow injury turned out to be serious. He needed surgery to repair a ligament. While Shohei was a great designated hitter during the 2019 season, he barely pitched. In 2020 he didn't pitch at all. Shohei's hitting suffered too. That year, his batting average was .190—he didn't get a hit about 80 percent of the time.

Luckily, 2021 was a different story. That season, Shohei showed everyone what he could do. He lived up to being called Japan's Babe Ruth. In fact, he had one of the best seasons in baseball history. Finally allowed to hit

Shohei is the first MLB player since Babe Ruth to dominate as both a pitcher and a hitter.

ANGELS
17

on days he pitched, Shohei appeared in the batting lineup every day. In 155 games, he had 46 homers, 138 base hits, 100 RBIs, 26 **stolen bases**, and an OPS of .965. As a pitcher he had 156 strikeouts in 23 starts. He won several awards in 2021, including MLB Player of the Year, AL Silver Slugger, AL MVP, and the MLB Commissioner's Historic Achievement Award. He was also voted by fans and players to appear in the All-Star Game.

Shohei continued to show his talents in 2022 and 2023, dominating as a hitter and pitcher. In 2023, Shohei competed in the World Baseball Classic for Team Japan. He struck out MLB superstar Mike Trout to get the win for his team and took home yet another MVP award.

By the end of 2023, Shohei was the league's most exciting **free agent**. At age 29, he signed a ten-year contract with the Los Angeles Dodgers. It was the largest contract in sports history—$700 million. Before that, the biggest contract ever signed by an athlete was $450 million!

ZOOM IN: THE GREATS ON THE G.O.A.T.

"He's the most incredible athlete I've ever seen in baseball," said Houston Astros manager Dusty Baker. "He can outrun a deer. He can throw a hundred miles an hour, hit a ball a mile."

"He's got the best stuff in the league," said MLB superstar Mike Trout. "I don't think I've talked to anybody . . . that wants to face that dude."

"We should make a new award for him," said Boston Red Sox manager Alex Cora. "This is something MLB hasn't seen since Babe Ruth."

"MVP with ease," said Chicago Cubs pitcher Marcus Stroman. "What he's doing is insane."

Shohei and his teammates meet with President Trump after their World Series victory.

Back in Los Angeles for the 2024 baseball season, Shohei now wore the Dodgers' blue-and-white uniform. He couldn't pitch because of another elbow injury, but he set several baseball records, wowing the world with his talent as a hitter and base runner. He even helped the Dodgers win the World Series. With a giant championship ring on his finger, Shohei had fulfilled his lifelong dream.

But not everything was going well for Shohei. Through all the glory, he also faced setbacks and controversies.

NHK
ANGELS

CHAPTER 3:

Major-League Pains

Shohei had undoubtedly earned the respect and admiration of the professional baseball world. He was doing what no other player had done since Babe Ruth. And Shohei was doing it better.

But not everything was going his way. The trouble started when Shohei made the leap to MLB. Some people said he was the new face of baseball. But not everyone thought he was the best person for the job.

"This brother is special, make no mistake about it," said sports journalist Stephen A. Smith on the sports channel ESPN. "But . . . I don't think it helps that the number one face is a dude that needs an interpreter so that you can understand what the [heck] he's saying in this country."

Luckily, Shohei was unfazed. "I mean, if I could speak English, I would speak English," he said in an interview in Japanese. "There would only be positive things to come from that. But I came here to play baseball, at the end of the day, and I've felt like my play

Shohei's skills and knowledge make him a popular interviewee for news and sports broadcasts.

ZOOM IN: THE COST OF FAME

After Shohei's 2024 World Series with the Los Angeles Dodgers, the media rushed onto the field to get a quote from him. Usually, he is happy to give interviews. But there were some people he didn't want to talk to. Shohei refused to give interviews to Nippon TV and Fuji TV. That's because they had leaked Shohei's new home address in California. For his own safety and privacy, he was forced to sell his house before he even moved in. Though Fuji TV apologized, Shohei was angry. And he wasn't afraid to let those media outlets know it.

on the field could be my way of communicating with the people, with the fans."

Shohei wasn't stressed about being the "new face of baseball." "I'm actually happy to hear that," he said. "It's what I came here for, to be the best player I can. And hearing 'the face of baseball,' that's very welcoming to me . . . it gives me more motivation to keep it up, and have more great years."

But fame had its downside. "He hasn't really been able to go out freely since his rookie year with the Fighters," said Shohei's longtime translator Ippei Mizuhara. During the offseason in Japan, fans and media followed Shohei around. He had to move carefully from his

Shohei talks with media at DodgerFest 2024 with translator Ippei Mizuhara on his right.

house to a car and sneak into restaurants through the side door.

"I really feel like there's probably not one single person that can match his popularity right now," Ippei said. "I heard a lot of people say that Shohei himself was a bigger attraction than the Olympics in Japan. The best part of the pandemic. I hear a lot of people wake up to watching Shohei. He'll hit a home run and it'll just lighten up the whole country."

Ippei got Shohei into trouble before the start of the 2024 season. He accused Shohei of gambling on sports, which is illegal. After an investigation, the truth came out: Ippei had stolen $17 million from Shohei's bank account and used it to gamble on sports, telling people he was betting for Shohei. At a press conference, using a new interpreter, Shohei set the record straight. "I never bet on baseball or any other sport," he said. "I'm beyond shocked. It's hard to verbalize how I am feeling at this point."

Ippei pleaded guilty to bank and tax fraud and was sentenced to serve jail time. MLB declared that Shohei was "a victim of fraud and this matter has been closed." The Dodgers said they were "pleased that Shohei and the team can put this entire matter behind them and move forward in pursuit of a World Series title."

Shohei doesn't let his personal life affect his play.

LA
Los Angeles
17
LA

Through all his injuries and trials, Shohei keeps his smile and determination.

17
ANGELES

Coping with elbow and knee injuries was also hard for Shohei. It meant the dual player couldn't pitch for several seasons. "More than frustration it was disappointment," said Shohei about his injuries, "because I knew there were certain expectations that were surrounding me, and I wasn't able to meet those."

Even though he couldn't pitch, Shohei shone as a designated hitter. He even helped his team make it to the 2024 World Series. But injury struck again.

Coaches and trainers aid Shohei after his 2024 World Series injury.

ZOOM IN: THE WORLD SERIES PARADE

On November 1, 2024, more than 200,000 fans lined the parade route in Los Angeles to celebrate the Dodgers' World Series win. As the Dodgers' parade bus rolled along, Shohei said through his interpreter, "I'm totally overwhelmed with the amount of fans who are here . . . It's been an incredible year. I'm so happy that I was able to contribute." He also spoke to fans without an interpreter. "This is so special," Shohei said in English. "I'm so honored to be here. Congratulations, Los Angeles. Thank you, guys."

During game two of the World Series, Shohei hurt himself while trying to steal a base. Even so, the Dodgers went on to triumph over the New York Yankees. After the championship parade through the streets of Los Angeles, Shohei had surgery to repair torn tissue in his left shoulder. It was another big disappointment. The Dodgers' general manager, Brandon Gomes, gave an update on Shohei's recovery: "We're going to take it piece by piece and get through this and then take it in one-, two-week chunks and make sure that we're in a really good place on each of those benchmarks and then go from there and not try to say, 'Hey, we need to be ready by this day.' We're going to let the rehab process play out."

Shohei knows how easily a season can end. It's why he plays every game like it's his last. "[Baseball] is a job where you never know when you'll get seriously injured, and if it doesn't work out, you can just quit," he said. "That's why I want to be prepared for it to happen at any time, and live each day without regrets. I'm optimistic."

CHAPTER 4:

Home Base

Baseball fans around the world are curious about Shohei. They want to know what he eats, how he trains, and even how much he sleeps. Though he likes to keep some things private, Shohei has been happy to share a few aspects of his personal life.

For example, he was thrilled to introduce his dog Dekopin, or Decoy, to fans. In 2024, he brought the kooikerhondje on the field to throw out the opening pitch in a Dodgers versus Orioles game. Shohei and Decoy appeared together as a bobblehead toy. And of course, Decoy rode the Dodgers' bus with Shohei during the World Series parade. The media named Decoy the MVP of the series—most valuable pet.

During the 2024 offseason, while Shohei was recovering from elbow surgery, he talked about Decoy. "I originally wanted to have a dog, but (that desire) seems to have been accelerated by the

Shohei and his dog ride in a double-decker bus in a parade through Los Angeles to celebrate the world championship.

ZOOM IN: FRIENDS FOREVER

Shohei easily makes friends with his MLB teammates. He often laughs and jokes around with them in the dugout. One of his first friends in MLB was Angels superstar Mike Trout. Trout would often tease Shohei, treating him like a little brother. The two hit back-to-back in the lineup, so fans called them Troutani. Shohei's best friend on the Dodgers is said to be pitcher Yoshinobu Yamamoto. Shohei also pals around with right fielder Teoscar Hernández, who is from the Dominican Republic. They joke around in English and help each other learn Japanese and Spanish.

surgery. Now it's a dog and rehabilitation. That's all I have . . . I'm always with him when I'm training and running."

Another dream Shohei had was to get married. In a February 2024 Instagram post, Shohei announced that this dream had come true. "Not only have I began a new chapter in my career with the Dodgers but I also have began a new life with someone from my native country of Japan who is very special to me and I wanted everyone to know I am now married." On April 19, 2025, Shohei and his wife welcomed a baby daughter.

Shohei's wife, Mamiko Tanaka, played in the Women's Japan Basketball League from 2019 to 2023. While playing for a team called the Fujitsu Red Wave in 2022–2023, she averaged 24 minutes, 7.8 points, and 6.0 rebounds per game. In addition to playing professional basketball, she represented Japan at the international youth and college level. In one video on social media, the couple play basketball together. Shohei admits he's not the best at the sport.

When Shohei isn't with his family, he can be found training for baseball. His teammates say he works harder than anyone to be the

Shohei's jersey has topped MLB sales records for two seasons.

best he can be. It all begins with a good night's rest. Shohei makes sure to get 10 to 12 hours of sleep a day. He uses special pillows to ensure he's comfortable. After he wakes up, he heads out for six hours of training. He lifts weights, practices pitching, does hitting drills, and works on his agility, or ability to move quickly. He does everything with care and purpose. Shohei gets home from training around 2:00 or 3:00 p.m. He thinks about baseball even when he's not training. He focuses on eating healthy, resting, stretching, reviewing game footage, thinking about strategy, and analyzing how he played. He also naps and gets massages to make sure his body is in good shape.

Shohei's teammate Chris Taylor said, "His work ethic is second to none, he's super meticulous with everything he does. I don't think I've seen someone take so long in between

ZOOM IN: GOOD HABITS

Shohei's focus was always on baseball, even before he was an MLB star. While living in the dorms with his Fighters teammates, Shohei never went out drinking. If he wasn't training, he was playing video games, working out, or reading books on how to improve. One MLB scout said, "He didn't care about anything else, it seemed, than getting better at baseball. To Shohei, everything revolved around baseball and how to get better at it." That dedicated focus and determination stayed the same as Shohei joined the big leagues. His work ethic has definitely paid off.

OHTANI
17

each and every rep, because he puts that much focus into it. Whether he's doing dry swings in the cage or sprint work out on the field, he's literally creating a game situation. He'll have 20 dry swings in the cage and it's gonna take him 20 minutes because he's gonna take a minute in between every swing to visualize the situation. He's gonna step out, take his breaths. It's pretty special to watch, and I think that's why he's as good as he is."

"I want to still be playing baseball when I'm 39 or 40 years old . . . the day will come when I will retire, but when that time comes, I want to continue to love baseball."

While Shohei says he loves In-N-Out burgers, he mostly eats healthy. He spends his offseason in Japan, where he enjoys his mother's home cooking. He doesn't eat junk food or drink alcohol.

Shohei grew up reading a Japanese **manga** series called *Major.* It's about a character named Goro Honda, who pitches and hits. He even makes it all the way to MLB, just like Shohei. "Goro's passion made me love baseball even more," said Shohei about the series, which he still loves. In another interview, he said he likes the manga series *Slam Dunk*, about a basketball team that goes from meh to amazing.

Shohei also loves the Japanese art form **anime**. His favorite show is a famous anime series called *One Piece*. For the 2021 season, Shohei used the "Jujutsu Kaisen" anime theme as his **walk-up song**.

But he likes other music, too. He's had different walk-up songs that showcase his taste. When he was with the Angels, his walk-up songs included "Twinbow" by Slushii and Marshmello, "Do or Die" by Afrojack and Thirty Seconds to Mars, and the theme from *Game of Thrones*. During Shohei's first season with the Dodgers, his walk-up song was "The Show Goes On" by Lupe Fiasco.

Shohei keeps getting better and better. He sets an admirable example for teammates and fans. And he does it because he wants to be the best he can be for as long as he can. "I want to still be playing baseball when I'm 39 or 40 years old," he said in an interview. "If possible, I'd like to stay active. Of course, the day will come when I will retire, but when that time comes, I want to continue to love baseball."

When Shohei was little, he kept a list of his goals in his diary. He wanted to play MLB. He wanted to win the World Series and get married. And he dreams of coaching his own children one day. So far, Shohei has achieved most of his goals. There's not telling what one of the best baseball players in the world will do next.

Highlight Reels

A HEART OF GOLD

Shohei is as generous and compassionate as he is talented. Over the years, he's supported many meaningful causes. In 2020, during the COVID-19 pandemic, he donated masks to healthcare workers through the Japan Mask Project. In 2021, after participating in the All-Star Game Home Run Derby, he donated his winnings—$150,000—to about 30 support staff with the Los Angeles Angels. It was his way of thanking them for their help during his first years in MLB. Two years later, he donated 60,000 youth gloves to Japan's 20,000 elementary schools to help them develop a love for baseball. When a series of earthquakes struck Japan's western coast on January 1, 2024, Shohei and his new team, the Los Angeles Dodgers, donated more than $1 million to help victims. Hundreds of people died or went missing. In a social media post, Shohei wrote, "I would like to thank those who have joined in the recovery effort, and my hope is that we continue to come together to support those whose lives have been upended. I hope for the rapid rescue of missing persons and the reconstruction of the disaster-stricken areas." In May 2024, sports fans were excited to see Shohei attend a special charity event with his wife, Mamiko. Though the two keep a low profile, they supported the annual Los Angeles Dodgers Blue Diamond Gala. Funds raised support community projects in the city.

SHO ME THE MONEY

When Shohei was 18, he signed with a Japanese professional baseball team called the Fighters. He received a rookie salary of 15 million yen, or about $131,000 USD, plus bonuses of about $1.3 million. When he switched to MLB at age 23, complicated rules meant he couldn't be paid a lot of money.

He was allowed to earn only a $3.5 million bonus and a salary of no more than $545,000 for three years. The Los Angeles Angels got him for a steal, though they had to pay his former Japanese team, the Fighters, a $20 million posting fee. In 2023, Shohei became a free agent, which meant teams could bid for him. And they did! In December 2023, Shohei made history. He signed a $700 million, ten-year contract with the Los Angeles Dodgers. It was the biggest deal in sports history. Shohei receives $2 million for each year of the contract. The rest—$680 million—will be paid out from 2034 to 2043. In each of those years, he will earn $68 million! His contract gives him a suite at Dodger Stadium for regular and postseason games. He also gets an interpreter, because he's still learning English. He earns about $40 million a year in endorsements, representing brands like New Balance and Japan Airlines. But winning—not money—is what motivates Shohei. In 2024, his first year with the Dodgers, Shohei and his teammates won the biggest prize in baseball: the World Series.

BIG IN JAPAN

Shohei isn't the first major league player to come from Japan. Fans will also know these amazing baseball heroes: Hideo Nomo, Masahiro Tanaka, Ichiro Suzuki, Hideki Matsui, and Yu Darvish. Shohei looked up to them all. While growing up, he watched power hitter Hideki Matsui play for Tokyo's Yomiuri Giants. Shohei wanted to hit like him. And when he got older, he loved working out with Yu Darvish, who helped Shohei gain 20 pounds (9 kilograms) of muscle before entering MLB. Today, Shohei is Japan's most recognizable star. That's because baseball is the country's most popular sport. It was introduced in the country in 1872, and Japan's first professional league started in the 1930s. By 1949, it had become Nippon Professional Baseball (NBP). The league now has 12 teams. NPB is the world's top baseball league after MLB. Japan also has the second highest level of attendance after the United States—about 25,000 fans per game. Team Japan has won several Olympic medals, including a gold in the 2021 Olympics. They worked hard to beat Team USA 2—0. And they won on their home turf: That year, the Olympics took place in Tokyo, Japan. Then, in March 2023 at the World Baseball Classic in Miami, Florida, Japan beat the United States 3-2 in a dramatic finish. Shohei was voted MVP of the tournament.

Glossary

American League—one of two leagues in Major League Baseball

anime—a style of Japanese film and television animation, typically aimed at adults as well as children

designated hitter—the player who bats for their team's pitcher during a baseball game

endorsements—when brands or companies pay someone to represent their products

free agent—player who isn't under contract with a team and is eligible to sign with another team

Japan Series—the annual championship series in Nippon Professional Baseball; a best-of-seven series played by the top teams in the Central and Pacific Leagues of NPB

Major League Baseball (MLB)—the highest level of professional baseball, with 30 teams in Canada and the United States

manga—a style of Japanese comic books and graphic novels, typically aimed at adults as well as children

National League— one of two leagues in Major League Baseball

posted—a process that lets Japanese players negotiate directly with MLB teams

OPS—on-base plus slugging percentage, a combination of a baseball player's on-base percentage and slugging percentage, meant to measure a player's performance at getting on base and power hitting

posting fee—a payment made by one organization to another that allows them to negotiate with a player

RBIs—runs batted in, or when a batter makes a hit that enables another runner on their team to score

stolen bases—when a base runner advances to the next base while the pitcher is throwing to the batter

walk-up song—a song that plays when a player walks up to home plate to bat

Selected Bibliography

"A Baseball Story to Watch," *60 Minutes*, Season 49 Episode 41, CBS News, June 23, 2017. cbs.com/shows/video/9E_glfYH_XPH7UicPYBvlOLsyTDvn4fV/.

Fletcher, Jeff, *Sho-Time: The Inside Story of Shohei Ohtani and the Greatest Baseball Season Ever Played*, Diversion Books, 2022.

Paris, Jay, *Shohei Ohtani: The Amazing Story of Baseball's Two-Way Japanese Superstar*, Sports Publishing, 2018.

Riley, Daniel, "How Shohei Ohtani Made Baseball Fun Again, *GQ Sports*, January 12, 2022. gq.com/story/shohei-ohtani-february-cover-profile.

Wertheim, Jon, "Shohei Ohtani: Japan's Babe Ruth," *60 Minutes Sports*, CBS News, June 20, 2021. cbsnews.com/news/shohei-ohtani-mlb-two-way-player-60-minutes-2021-06-20/.

Zwelling, Arden, "The Next Babe Ruth: How Shohei Ohtani became MLB's most dominant two-way player in a century," Sportsnet, 2017. sportsnet.ca/baseball/mlb/big-read-meet-shohei-otani-next-babe-ruth.

Websites

Shohei Ohtani

https://www.britannica.com/biography/Shohei-Ohtani
A brief biography of Ohtani.

Shohei Ohtani

https://www.espn.com/mlb/player/_/id/39832/shohei-ohtani
Learn about Ohtani's position, stats, etc.

Shohei Ohtani

https://www.mlb.com/player/shohei-ohtani-660271
Read key facts and news about Ohtani.

Index